CREATIVE EDUCATION

Published by Creative Education
123 South Broad Street
Mankato, Minnesota 56001
Creative Education is an imprint of The Creative Company.

DESIGN AND PRODUCTION BY EVANSDAY DESIGN

PHOTOGRAPHS BY Getty Images (Andrew D. Bernstein, TIMOTHY
CLARY / AFP, Jim Cummins / NBAE, Jerry Driendl, Allen Einstein /
NBAE, Jesse D. Garrabrant / NBAE, Walter Looss Jr. / NBAE, Neil
Leifer / NBAE, Robert Lewis / NBAE, Steve Lipofsky / NBAE, NBA
Photo Library / NBAE, NBA PHOTOS / NBAE, Rich Pilling / NBAE,
Ken Regan / NBAE, Ezra O. Shaw / ALLSPORT, Dale Tait / NBAE,
John G. Zimmerman / Time Life Pictures)

LIBRARY OF CONGRESS CATALOGING-IN-PUBLICATION DATA

LeBoutillier, Nate.
The story of the Philadelphia 76ers / by Nate LeBoutillier.
p. cm. — (The NBA—a history of hoops)
Includes index.
ISBN-13: 978-1-58341-420-0
1. Philadelphia 76ers (Basketball team)—History—
Juvenile literature. I. Title. II. Series.

GV885.52.P45L43 2006
796.323'64'0974811—dc22   2005051770

First edition

9 8 7 6 5 4 3 2 1

COVER PHOTO: *Allen Iverson*

THE STORY OF THE
PHILADELPHIA
76ERS

NATE LeBOUTILLIER

CREATIVE EDUCATION

It's 1983.

AND THE PHILADELPHIA SPECTRUM IS HUMMING.
76ERS FORWARD BOBBY JONES, ALL SWEAT AND
FLOORBURNS, GRABS A LOOSE BALL AND SHOVELS IT
TO FLEET-FOOTED GUARD MO CHEEKS. CHEEKS QUICKLY
OUTLETS THE BALL TO JULIUS "DR. J" ERVING, AND THE
CROWD JUMPS TO THEIR FEET. ERVING ZEROES IN ON
THE ONE DEFENDER BETWEEN HIM AND THE BASKET,
TAKES ONE LONG, LAST STRIDE, AND LEAPS INTO THE AIR.
THE DEFENDER DOESN'T HAVE A CHANCE. DR. J SWOOPS
IN LIKE A BREEZE, HIS RIGHT ARM WINDMILLING THE
BALL THROUGH THE RIM. THIS IS PHILADELPHIA 76ERS
BASKETBALL AT ITS FINEST.

PHILADELPHIA 76ERS
Philadelphia Pennsylvania

BIRTH OF THE SIXERS

EVEN THOUGH ITS NAME IS GREEK (MEANING "CITY of Brotherly Love"), and it founders were British, the city of Philadelphia, Pennsylvania, is American through and through. Philadelphia is where the Declaration of Independence was signed in 1776, where Benjamin Franklin established America's first public library and newspaper, and where the 76ers, whose name is symbolic of Philadelphia's place in American history, joined the National Basketball Association (NBA) in 1963.

9

Philadelphia's NBA history began with the Warriors, who won two league championships in 14 seasons

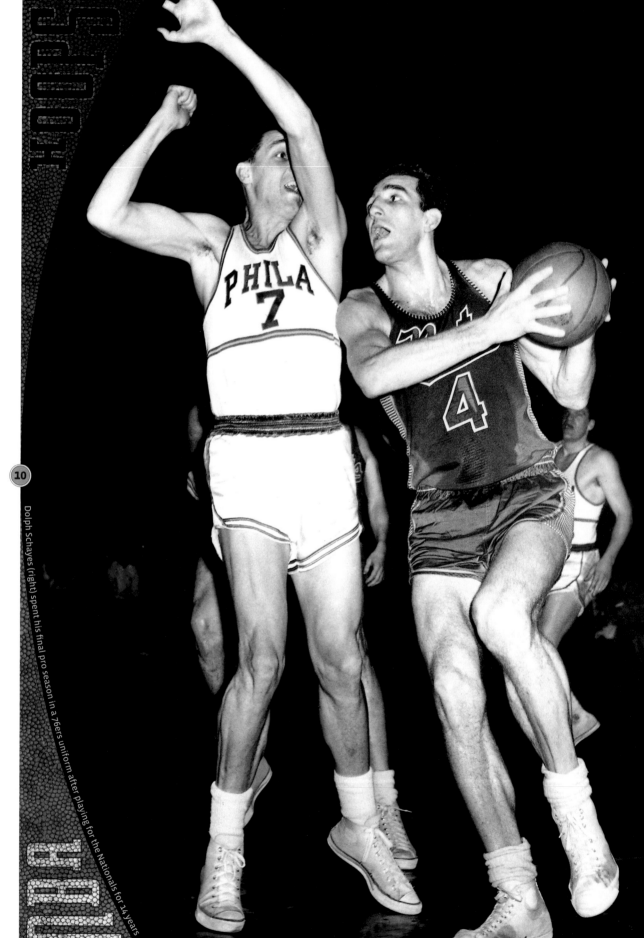

Dolph Schayes (right) spent his final pro season in a 76ers uniform after playing for the Nationals for 14 years

The history of pro basketball in Philadelphia actually began not with the 76ers, but with another team known as the Warriors. The Warriors were an original member of the Basketball Association of America (BAA), formed in 1946, and won the league's first championship. When the BAA merged with another league in 1949 to form the NBA, the Philadelphia Warriors became a charter member of the NBA.

The Warriors played in Philadelphia for 14 years, then moved to San Francisco in 1962. A year later, a team called the Syracuse Nationals relocated to Philadelphia and became the 76ers. The "new" team was led by two future Hall-of-Famers: high-scoring guard Hal Greer and hardworking forward Dolph Schayes. The 6-foot-9 Schayes was famous for his energy and determination. "I didn't have much speed, but I felt that by constantly moving, I could free myself," said Schayes. "I kept pushing myself. I saw myself never getting tired."

Greer, meanwhile, was an accurate jump shooter who even jumped before releasing the ball when he shot free throws. He was the club leader in every offensive category except rebounding, which was the domain of veteran center John Kerr and young forward Chet Walker.

HAL GREER, REGULAR GUY

The pages of the Philadelphia 76ers' photo album are eye-catching. There's a colorful photo of Dr. J flying acrobatically toward the rim. There's the multi-tattooed Allen Iverson snaking through the defense, his hair knotted into pristine cornrows. There's Moses Malone, sweat pouring from his face as he pounds the boards. A picture of Hal Greer, one of the steadiest guards in the history of the game, may go unnoticed because Greer, in 14 seasons with the franchise, was all business—a quietly steady teammate. "Hal Greer always came to play," Sixers great Dolph Schayes said upon Greer's 1981 induction into the Basketball Hall of Fame. "He came to practice the same way. Every bus and plane and train, he was on time. Hal Greer punched the clock. Hal Greer brought the lunch pail."

WILT BRINGS HOME A TITLE

THE 76ERS WERE SUCCESSFUL, BUT NOT CHAMPIONSHIP-caliber. That all changed when, in 1965, the club traded for local hero Wilt Chamberlain, who had played his high school basketball in "Philly." With the 7-foot-1 "Big Dipper" and power forward Luke Jackson, Philadelphia was suddenly a championship contender.

13

Wilt Chamberlain combined extraordinary size and quickness to become a force of legendary proportions

Billy Cunningham enjoyed a Hall of Fame playing career and later became head coach of the 76ers

PHILA 32

Billy Cunningham arrived in Philadelphia via the 1966 NBA Draft. A 6-foot-7 forward from the University of North Carolina, Cunningham was nicknamed "The Kangaroo Kid" for his great jumping ability and aggressiveness, and he brought new fire to the 76ers lineup that opened the 1966–67 season.

Under new coach Alex Hannum, the club finished with a 68–13 record, the best mark in NBA history up to that time. The mighty 76ers breezed by the Cincinnati Royals and Boston Celtics in the first two rounds of the playoffs, then wrapped up the NBA title by trouncing Chamberlain's old team—the San Francisco Warriors—in six games. At last, Chamberlain had helped bring an NBA title home to Philadelphia. "The fact that I had the honor to coach that team is the reason I'm in the Hall of Fame," Coach Hannum would say years later.

The 76ers continued on in 1967–68 as if their championship year had never ended, finishing the season with a 62–20 record. But the Celtics, led by stars Bill Russell and John Havlicek, roared back from a three-games-to-one deficit to beat the 76ers in the Eastern Conference Finals, then captured their 10th NBA championship in 12 years.

WILT'S WEAKNESS

Even the great ones have a weakness. For Hall of Fame center Wilt Chamberlain, it was free-throw shooting. In his four seasons with the 76ers, Chamberlain actually got worse at the free-throw line each season, making a mere 38 percent in 1967–68, his last year in Philadelphia. Chamberlain tried many different styles at the foul line, shooting farther back from the 15-foot line, or from the right or left corners. He even shot free throws "granny style" to try to shake things up. Although he made just 51 percent for his career, Chamberlain made 28 of 32 free throws in his record-setting 100-point game on March 2, 1962, while playing for the Philadelphia Warriors. "I wasn't even thinking of hitting 100," said Chamberlain, "but after putting in 9 straight free throws, I was thinking about a foul-shooting record."

DR. J HEALS THE PAIN

THE 1968 CONFERENCE FINALS LOSS SENT THE 76ERS into a terrible downward spiral. Over the next two seasons, Coach Hannum resigned, Chamberlain was traded to the Los Angeles Lakers, and Cunningham signed with an American Basketball Association (ABA) team. In 1972–73, the 76ers finished 9–73, which remains the worst record in NBA history.

One of the strongest men in the NBA, George McGinnis averaged 11 boards a game for Philadelphia

Julius Erving pioneered an "above-the-rim" playing style later embraced by such stars as Michael Jordan

Things changed for the better in the summer of 1975, when the 76ers signed forward George McGinnis. In 1975–76, McGinnis, a former ABA Most Valuable Player (MVP), led the 76ers in scoring and rebounding. A year later, the Sixers purchased the contract of forward Julius "Dr. J" Erving from the financially troubled New Jersey Nets of the ABA. With his amazing fakes and soaring dunks, Erving put on an impressive show. Said former NBA star Dave DeBusschere, "There are athletes who are known as 'the franchise,' but Julius isn't the franchise—he's the league!"

Erving's arrival was a turning point for the 76ers, and with McGinnis, he led the 76ers to the Eastern Conference crown in 1976–77. But the Portland Trail Blazers and their star center, Bill Walton, ended their championship hopes in the 1977 NBA Finals.

The following year, McGinnis was traded to the Denver Nuggets for forward Bobby Jones, a fierce and unselfish defender and rebounder. Philadelphia also drafted 6-foot-3 point guard Maurice "Mo" Cheeks, who instantly became the floor general of Philadelphia's dangerous ball club.

THE POWER OF CHOCOLATE THUNDER

Forward Darryl Dawkins didn't just have a crazy nickname ("Chocolate Thunder"), he gave crazy nicknames to his slam dunks. There was the Yo Mama. The Rim Wrecker. The Spine Chiller Supreme. But on November 13, 1979, in Kansas City, Dawkins power-slammed the ball so hard that he tore the rim off and shattered the backboard, with shards of glass nicking up his defender, Royals forward Bill Robinzine, and lodging in teammate Julius Erving's afro. He titled it, *The Chocolate-Thunder-Flying, Robinzine-Crying, Teeth-Shaking, Glass-Breaking, Rump-Roasting, Bun-Toasting, Wham-Bam, Glass-Breaker-I-Am-Jam*. Two weeks later, he broke another backboard. "I didn't mean to destroy it," said Dawkins, who was a 76ers player from 1975 to 1982. "It was the power, the Chocolate Thunder. I could feel it surging through my body, fighting to get out. I had no control over it."

TO THE TOP AGAIN

IN 1980–81, ERVING BECAME THE FIRST NON-CENTER to win the NBA's MVP award in 17 years, averaging 24.6 points, 8 rebounds, and 4.4 assists per game and leading Philly to a 62–20 record, tied for best in the league. "He was alive again this season," said Kevin Loughery, the coach of the Atlanta Hawks. "He was the Dr. J of old, the one I saw and coached in the old ABA. He was a lot wiser, sometimes less flamboyant, but awesome again."

21

Maurice Cheeks's fierce defense and terrific on-court leadership made him a four-time NBA All-Star

Hall of Fame center Moses Malone spent the prime seasons of his 21-year professional career in Philadelphia

Even with Dr. J at the top of his game, though, the Sixers lost to the Los Angeles Lakers in the 1982 NBA Finals. That off-season, the 76ers traded with the Houston Rockets for center Moses Malone. Some critics wondered whether Erving would be able to share the spotlight with Malone, a two-time NBA MVP. Dr. J had no such doubts. "At this point, winning the title is the only thing that's on my mind," he said.

Erving and Malone powered the Sixers to 65 victories during the 1982–83 season. Cat-quick shooting guard Andrew Toney teamed with Cheeks in the backcourt, and Jones and forward Marc Iavaroni took care of the defensive and rebounding dirty work. The 76ers waltzed through the playoffs with ease and then swept the Lakers in the Finals. Malone was named MVP of both the regular season and the Finals, and Erving proudly hoisted the NBA championship trophy over his head while Philadelphia fans celebrated.

It was a fleeting moment of glory, however. With virtually the same squad, the next three years saw the 76ers flounder at playoff time. Eventually, Malone was traded away, Toney succumbed to injuries, and Erving and Jones retired. Soon, only Cheeks was left from the 76ers' championship squad, but he was not alone as the club leader. Joining him was one of the most unusual talents in NBA history: forward Charles Barkley.

THE GREATEST SHOT EVER?

The Lakers were leading the 76ers in the 1980 NBA Finals, two games to one, and Philadelphia fans were desperate for a win. Late in the fourth quarter of Game 4, the teams were neck-and-neck. In this tense situation, 76ers forward Julius Erving pulled off perhaps the greatest shot the NBA had ever seen. Erving beat his man to the baseline and leaped high on the right side of the basket. The only problem was that 7-foot-2 Lakers center Kareem Abdul-Jabbar was still in the way. "Dr. J" somehow swooped under the basket and flicked the ball in on the other side. "My mouth just dropped open," said Lakers guard Magic Johnson. "I thought, 'What should we do? Should we take the ball out, or should we ask him to do it again?'"

25

Andrew Toney's (with ball) great play against the rival Celtics earned him the nickname "The Boston Strangler"

SIR CHARLES AND THE ANSWER

THE 6-FOOT-5 AND 280-POUND BARKLEY, DRAFTED in 1984, looked more like a football lineman than a basketball star, but he was a fierce competitor who outfought and outjumped taller opponents. He also outtalked them, never lacking something interesting to say. "If I weren't earning $3 million a year to dunk a basketball," Barkley once said, "most people on the street would run in the other direction if they saw me coming."

The 76ers put together winning records in six of Barkley's eight seasons in Philadelphia, and "Sir Charles" averaged 23 points and nearly 12 rebounds per game in those years. But Philadelphia always stumbled in the playoffs. Barkley finally asked to be traded in 1992, and was, to the Phoenix Suns.

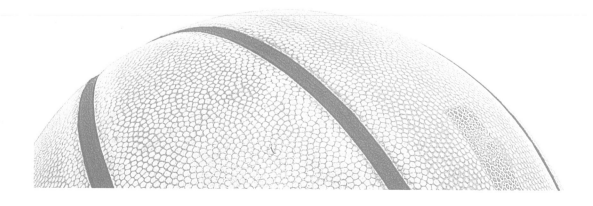

27

No player in the NBA attacked the rim more aggressively than one-of-a-kind forward Charles Barkley

Fearless and unbelievably quick point guard Allen Iverson captured the NBA MVP award in 2000–01

As Philadelphia fans watched Barkley win the league MVP award in 1992–93 and lead Phoenix to the NBA Finals, the 76ers sank in the standings. In 1995–96, they finished 18–64. The good news was that the 76ers "won" the right to pick first in the 1996 NBA Draft, and they selected Georgetown University point guard Allen Iverson. Nicknamed "The Answer," Iverson announced that he planned to be the answer to Philadelphia's quest for another NBA title.

Iverson backed up his talk with action. The lightning-quick guard proved that he could break down opposing defenses better than anyone else in the league. "I try to put pressure on the defense," Iverson explained. "I am always, always looking to score, always looking to make something happen on the court."

Before the 1997–98 season, the 76ers persuaded longtime NBA coach Larry Brown to come to Philly to rebuild the club around Iverson. The acquisition of big man Dikembe Mutombo and hustling guard Eric Snow improved the team's defense, and in 2000–01, the rebuilt Sixers surged all the way

TATTOOS IN BASKETBALL

People have been intentionally marking their skin as a form of decoration since perhaps the beginning of mankind. In America's short history, tattoos have usually been associated with sailors or other tough guys. But beginning in the 1990s, tattoos became more common, especially among athletes. The 76ers' Allen Iverson is one of the NBA's most famously tattooed players—and controversial figures. In 2001, *Sports Illustrated* featured him on the cover of its magazine, but airbrushed the tattoos off of his arms, legs, and neck. "It was an insult," Iverson said. "I wish they wouldn't use me at all if they can't accept all of me. I have things on my body that mean a lot to me, about my mother, my grandmother, my kids, my fiancée. These aren't just tattoos to me."

to the NBA Finals, where they faced the Lakers. Iverson scored 48 points as the 76ers took Game 1, but the Lakers rebounded to win the next four games and the NBA title.

Larry Brown stepped down as coach in 2003, and a succession of coaches followed. Iverson continued to score points in bunches, but the 76ers were a mediocre team. Things began looking up, though, as they drafted promising young forwards Samuel Dalembert (in 2001) and Andre Iguodala (2004), and traded for an excellent young three-point shooter in Kyle Korver (2003). Near the end of the 2004–05 season, Philadelphia also swapped players with the Sacramento Kings for veteran forward Chris Webber.

Along with these roster moves came a coaching change. In 2005, the 76ers returned to their roots, introducing their 1983 championship team's point guard, Maurice Cheeks, as the new head coach. "I welcomed the call," Cheeks said. "The people here in Philadelphia are sports people."

The Philadelphia 76ers have put together a long and proud history in the NBA, from the days of the 1983 Sixers, powered by Dr. J, to the current squad led by star guard Allen Iverson. With their recent revolutionary changes, the 76ers aim to make like America, forging their way to bigger and better things—namely, another NBA championship.

31

Rising star Andre Iguodala appeared in the starting lineup for every game of his rookie season in 2004–05

INDEX